MIX
Papier aus verantwortungsvollen Quellen
Paper from responsible sources
FSC® C105338

Samuel Jung

Sustainable Prosperity Through Qualitative Growth

An Economic Analysis Using the Example Of China

Anchor Compact

Jung, Samuel: Sustainable Prosperity Through Qualitative Growth: An Economic Analysis Using The Example Of China. Hamburg, Anchor Academic Publishing 2014
Original title of the thesis: Clinical Reasoning in der Altenpflege

Buch-ISBN: 978-3-95489-281-5
PDF-eBook-ISBN: 978-3-95489-781-0
Druck/Herstellung: Anchor Academic Publishing, Hamburg, 2014

Bibliografische Information der Deutschen Nationalbibliothek:
Die Deutsche Nationalbibliothek verzeichnet diese Publikation in der Deutschen Nationalbibliografie; detaillierte bibliografische Daten sind im Internet über http://dnb.d-nb.de abrufbar

Bibliographical Information of the German National Library:
The German National Library lists this publication in the German National Bibliography. Detailed bibliographic data can be found at: http://dnb.d-nb.de

All rights reserved. This publication may not be reproduced, stored in a retrieval system or transmitted, in any form or by any means, electronic, mechanical, photocopying, recording or otherwise, without the prior permission of the publishers.

Das Werk einschließlich aller seiner Teile ist urheberrechtlich geschützt. Jede Verwertung außerhalb der Grenzen des Urheberrechtsgesetzes ist ohne Zustimmung des Verlages unzulässig und strafbar. Dies gilt insbesondere für Vervielfältigungen, Übersetzungen, Mikroverfilmungen und die Einspeicherung und Bearbeitung in elektronischen Systemen.

Die Wiedergabe von Gebrauchsnamen, Handelsnamen, Warenbezeichnungen usw. in diesem Werk berechtigt auch ohne besondere Kennzeichnung nicht zu der Annahme, dass solche Namen im Sinne der Warenzeichen- und Markenschutz-Gesetzgebung als frei zu betrachten wären und daher von jedermann benutzt werden dürften.

Die Informationen in diesem Werk wurden mit Sorgfalt erarbeitet. Dennoch können Fehler nicht vollständig ausgeschlossen werden und die Diplomica Verlag GmbH, die Autoren oder Übersetzer übernehmen keine juristische Verantwortung oder irgendeine Haftung für evtl. verbliebene fehlerhafte Angaben und deren Folgen.

Alle Rechte vorbehalten

© Anchor Academic Publishing, ein Imprint der Diplomica® Verlag GmbH
http://www.diplom.de, Hamburg 2014
Printed in Germany

Table of Content

List of Figures II
List of Abbreviations III
    Brief Summary IV
    1. Introduction and leading question 1
    2. The notion of economic growth and prosperity 2
       2.1 Economic growth in terms of quantity and quality 2
       2.2 Measuring economic growth 5
       2.3 Political and social dimension of economic growth 7
       2.4 Innovation 9
       2.5 How to measure innovation 12
       2.6 Prosperity and sustainable development 12
    3. Striving for economic growth 17
    3.1 Potential dynamics and structure dynamics 17
       3.2 Qualitative Growth 18
    4. China's economic rise – potentials and threats 21
       4.1 Return of a world power 21
       4.2 Threats to China's prosperity 24
       4.3 China's potential for sustainable prosperity 26
       4.4 Interpretation and outlook 27
    5. Conclusion 28
    List of References 31

List of Figures

1 Subjective well-being by level of economic development 14
2 OECD and Non-OECD Energy Consumption 16
3 Hourly compensation costs of manufacturing employees in selected economies and
   regions 23

List of Abbreviations

CPC	Communist Party of China
EU	European Union
FDI	Foreign Direct Investment
GDP	Gross Domestic Product
GNP	Gross National Product
OECD	Organization for Economic Co-Operation and Development
PPP	Purchasing Power Parity
RMB	Renminbi
UNO	United Nations Organization
USA	United States of America

Brief Summary

This study with the title *Sustainable Prosperity Through Qualitative Growth – An Economic Analysis Using The Example Of China* analyzes the theoretical framework of economic growth and how it leads to sustainable prosperity. It propounds the notion of prosperity and sustainable development and thus explains the social, ecological and subsequently political dimension of economic growth.

The found insights are applied to the real-life example of the Chinese economic development of the past three decades to draw conclusions and explain why prosperity can be sustainable and which way leads to this goal.

1. Introduction and leading question

The Western world has seen tremendous growth in economic output and also national wealth: All of that started, as we know, with the Industrial Revolution in Great Britain in the second half of the 18th century. Drivers of this dramatic change were technological innovations like the steam engine or the spinning jenny. Thus manufacturers were enabled to multiply their output and produce every single item in a precisely alike manner, which manual production processes could not achieve in the very same way. So they were not only able to produce more but also produce with a higher and consistent quality. The new factories offered work and income to a vast number of peasants, who had before been caught in a feudal agricultural production system. That led to a sharp increase in per capita income and produced national wealth for the first time in history.

This book with the title "Sustainable Prosperity Through Qualitative Growth – An Economic Analysis Using The Example Of China" is aiming at propounding what economic growth means in terms of quantity and quality. The paper shall clarify what the drivers of economic growth are and will also deal with what the impacts to society and the environment are, when the economy starts to grow in the way it did in 18th century England.

The role of innovation is apparently a crucial one and this thesis shall thus explain how technological progress influences the economic output.

The paper starts with laying the theoretical basis and explaining and defining important terms and notions. This is necessary to understand what this thesis is actually about. Subsequently we go deeper into the topic of qualitative growth.

The example of China will be used to apply the found insights. For that China's current economic, social, scientific and political situation, including the author's personal experiences in the country, shall be analyzed and described to draw conclusions for its outlook: Will China be able to achieve sustainable prosperity and can prosperity be sustainable?

2. The notion of economic growth and prosperity

Throughout the years the public established a way of usually ranking countries by their income rather than for instance the social or political system. We speak of low income, middle and high income countries[1] or in other words developing, emerging and industrialized countries. The sole focus lies on GDP, the Gross Domestic Product, which defines the value of all goods and services produced by the production factors located within a country within a certain period[2]. The general notion is, that higher economic growth leads to higher income and prosperity and thus to high quality of life. But Bhutan, a small kingdom, located between India and Tibet, embedded Gross National Happiness into its constitution, to foster the growth of satisfaction instead of simply producing more, hoping to thus achieve happiness[3]. We thus need to question the classical notion of solely defining wealth and prosperity in material terms.

2.1 Economic growth in terms of quantity and quality

This paper's title names *economic growth* as an instrument of striving for prosperity. The term of economic growth describes a change in an economy's output; with output being the sum of the value all goods and services produced[4]. That brings us back to GDP, meaning that economic growth is the change in GDP. If the change is positive, we speak of growth and shrinkage in the opposite case. Another phenomenon is stagnation, which takes place, when the change in output is very small or zero[5].

We shall here use the term Gross Domestic Product instead of Gross National Product (GNP), because economic changes do not only happen within national borders, but also regions or special political, economic or financial zones, like the Euro zone. So observations of economic growth can be made for different groups that are linked in a way. GNP and GDP basically have the same meaning, with GNP restricting observations to nations; we are going to come back to that in 2.2.

Economic growth – be it positive or negative growth – is a continuous phenomenon. Thus economic growth is simply a change in output compared to a previous point in time[4].

---

[1] Cf. The World Bank Group (2012) a
[2] Weil (2005), p. 5
[3] Coen, A. (02.12.2011), 40,9 Prozent sind schon glücklich, ZEIT Online
[4] Cf. Oppenländer (1988), p.1
[5] Cf. Oppenländer (1988), p.1 et seq.

Changes in growth in the short term are economic trends or trade cycles[6]. Trends and growth are separate terms, although trends depict growth in the short term. Trends appear cyclically and fluctuate stronger, whilst growth is a rather steady process. We thus have to integrate economic trends into our observations, when describing economic growth.

When we speak of economic growth, we mean absolute changes in the GDP's value[7] compared to a previous period, so quantitative changes. Expressed in a mathematical equation we express growth as follows:

$$g = \frac{x_{t+1} - x_t}{x_t} \quad [8]$$

Economic growth (g) is therefor the change in the economy's output (x) from a previous period (t) to the following one (t+1). From that equation we can derive more information. If the economy has a constant growth rate g for a number of n years we rearrange for x_{t+1} and obtain:

$$x_{t+1} = x_t \times (1+g)^n \quad [8]$$

To calculate the average growth rate we obviously need to know the economy's output x in all periods considered and fill them into:

$$g = \left(\frac{x_{t+1}}{x_t}\right)^{1/n} - 1 \quad [8]$$

Let us now apply these formulas to the economy of Germany using data from the time span 2007 up until 2011[9]. We use the year 2007 as the base year x_t and 2011 will be x_{t+1}. The output x is represented in total GDP in current US$. We obtain the growth rate

$$g = \frac{3{,}570{,}555{,}555{,}556 - 3{,}323{,}807{,}412{,}152}{3{,}323{,}807{,}412{,}152}$$

$$g = 0.074 \approx 7\%$$

and an average growth rate of

$$g = \left(\frac{3{,}570{,}555{,}555{,}556}{3{,}323{,}807{,}412{,}152}\right)^{1/5} - 1$$

$$g = 0.014 \approx 1.4\% .$$

---

[6] Cf. Oppenländer (1988), p.3
[7] Cf. Oppenländer (1988), p.2
[8] Weil (2005), p. 10
[9] The World Bank Group (2012) b

It can be concluded that the German economy grew by around 7% from 2007 to 2011 with an average annual rate of 1.4%.

The growth that we calculated here determines change in the value of the economy's output. But value can either be increased by simply raising quantity, so producing more, or increasing the quality of products and services provided. Higher quality means higher value, which can be obtained by for example designing products more efficient, like engines, or extending a product's useful life. The data provided and used in the above example calculation do not explain explicitly, whether the growth was solely produced in a qualitative or quantitative way. That is reasoned as economic growth is a steady structural mutation or change in economic units[10] from enterprises and sectors to entire economies. Consequently economic growth comprises quantitative and qualitative changes. While one company improves quality and thus value of its products, demand and subsequently supply for another sector rise. Structural changes are an endless process resulting from consumer and producer behavior and new inventions[11]. We can see that in our saturated Western societies, where a new product like Apple's iPad causes absolutely new demands. What Oppenländer does not consider are the predictions published by the Club of Rome[12], a group of like-minded personalities with scientific or economic background, in 1972 under the title *The Limits to Growth*. The publication aroused big attention all over the world, because the group put the illusion of endless material growth to an end, because the world's natural resources are very obviously limited. Oppenländer's theory of endless growth has its limits, when it comes to material resources. It is evident, that structural changes can lead to unlimited economic changes and thus to growth, but this economic growth can in the very long run not only be based on quantitative growth. One cannot produce more and more, while the resources used become lesser and lesser. That leads us to the conclusion that economic growth must in the long run mutate to qualitative growth to last.

The descriptions of 2.1 assume an open market economy, where supply and demand are dynamic processes mostly conducted by the market agents. We do not want to ignore other types of economies, as they are also able to achieve economic growth. Planned economies, where the entire production and allocation is centrally planned by the government or a

---

[10] Oppenländer (1988), p.1
[11] Oppenländer (1988), p. 2
[12] The Club of Rome (2012), The story of the Club of Rome

government agency, can also face economic growth. Historically seen was the typical instrument is a five-year-plan, like the ones in the former Soviet Union. These plans prescribe precisely quantitative goals, like for example the length of new railway tracks or the minimum economic growth. Another type is the mixed economy with free markets or sectors but strong governmental control and/or planning. We are going to discuss that further in chapter 4.

2.2 Measuring economic growth

Measuring economic growth is everything but easy. As described in 2.1 is economic growth a dynamic and steady process, where sectors or companies as well as demand grow or shrink, new ones appear, while others disappear. This structural change must somehow be measured to be able to determine the rate, by which the economy grows. Precise growth rates simply do not exist.

Oppenländer names two different ways of measuring economic trends[13]. The *Inner Method* by Wald reads mathematical regularities or natural rules from past growth trends and thus predicts future developments. The second and more suitable method uses the production factors and includes exogenous and endogenous factors to construct a more dynamic model to measure growth.

In 2.1 we calculated growth rates using Gross Domestic Product. This must clearly be delimited from Gross National Product. When the German car producer Volkswagen produces and sells cars in China, it contributes to GDP in China and GNP in Germany. Volkswagen uses production factors owned by Chinese nationals, who earn an income from the production activity in China. But as Volkswagen is of German nationality the income the company earns from selling the cars contributes to German GNP.

The more popular concept is the one of GDP, because it presents the economic output in geographical areas, ignoring the producer's nationality, whereas GNP is a great index when it comes to tracing a nation's economic activities and its successes, which is helpful in a globalized economic environment.

Coming back to GDP: Here we have the choice between using real or nominal GDP. The calculations in 2.1 were based on current prices within one economy, which is the nominal GDP. That makes the nominal GDP dependent on the inflation rate, as it is directly linked to

---

[13] Cf. Oppenländer (1988), p. 4

the latest price level developments. This means that a 2% increase in inflation leads to a 2% increase in nominal GDP. Therefor it is rather common to use real GDP to depict economic growth because for its calculation the price level of a base year is used and makes the GDP's development over time comparable. The concept of real GDP is thus more suitable for calculating economic growth. Crucial instruments for achieving comparability are the Consumer Price Index, depicting the amount of inflation, and the GDP deflator, which simply brings prices down to the level of the chosen base year[14].

These ways are helpful when measuring economic growth within one economy respectively one currency zone. But comparing the economic developments between two different ones brings up new difficulties, because we now have to mind the exchange rates between the compared economy's currencies. Problem here is that exchange rates vary tremendously on a daily basis, without economic output changing at the same pace, which leads to distortions. A further issue arises from the fact that some goods are traded on international markets at common prices, so that in a relatively poorer country the traded good is more expansive than non-traded goods in the same country, because the *Law Of One* price states that a good must cost the same all over the world. But for that reason economically poorer countries are overstated, because they appear to be richer, because of these traded goods counting into their GDP[15].

The concept of *Purchasing Power Parity exchange rates* (PPP) avoids the two problems described above in creating a group of "artificial exchange rates [...], which are based on the prices of a standardized basket of goods and services (both traded and nontraded)[16]". That makes PPP also helpful for comparing other quantities than GDP.

But GDP itself does not say a lot about how materially wealthy a country's population actually is, as it only states the sum of all goods and services produced. When we compare a the GDP of Germany with 82 million inhabitants with the GDP of Austria with around 8 million people, we could conclude that Austria is poorer, because its GDP is so much lower. Therefor we need a more informative measurement, which is *Income per Capita*, where income stands for GDP. With income per capita we measure how much of the total GDP a single person on average obtains and can from that derive how materially "rich" or "poor"

---

[14] Cf. Weil (2005), p.24
[15] Cf. Weil (2005), p.25
[16] Weil (2005), p.25

the population is. Total GDP and GDP per capita have both advantages, depending on what we want to find out from our observations[17].

2.3 Political and social dimension of economic growth

When we discuss growth, we talk about very abstract processes that involve institutions, regulations and frameworks; formulas describe their act in combination and outcomes. What the theory usually neglects is that these processes affect people's life and their living conditions.

Economic growth usually leads to prosperity, which can better living conditions for a vast number of people - in the best case for the entire population. But to strive for growth we need people contributing their workforce, their skills and capital. We need natural resources, which are scarce and thus rivaling. Prof. Oppenländer sifts out six arguments for and against economic growth: Growth is wealth-multiplying, conflict-reducing, aim-fulfilling, environmentally harmful, dehumanizing, equality-retarding[18]. These arguments prove that growth is by far more than an economic phenomenon. It is also a social and political phenomenon and thus a political task. Politicians dedicating to economic growth do not only take over responsibility for a company's profit, but also for that companies employees, the natural resources used , so for the external effects to environment and society.

Oppenländer states that people's desires and needs can never be satisfied. With growing income or the satisfaction of existing needs new needs and desires arise, which causes the economy to continue growing[19]. We need to take into consideration that materially owning and consuming more does not automatically mean a higher degree of happiness. Happiness arises from the satisfaction of immaterial needs, like family and friendship, leisure, a fair and peaceful society and others[20].

We can conclude that material wealth is not an appropriate indicator of a society's prosperity. Prosperity is rather a mélange of the satisfaction of material and immaterial needs. That is why the United Nations Organization (UNO) started publishing the Human Development Index in their annual Human Development Report in 1990[21]. This index shall present a country's development stage by considering factors, that directly represent the

---

[17] Cf. Weil (2005), p.7
[18] Oppenländer (1988), p.171
[19] Cf. Oppenländer (1988), p.172
[20] Cf. Zabel (2011), p.38
[21] Cf. United Nations Organization, Human Development Reports (2012)

level of living standard, as for example the availability of food and clean water, education, safety, health care and many more. The result comes very close to being a well representative index, although the weighting of the factors is questionable. Availability of food is not as important in the well-off OECD-countries, but plays an essential role in the everyday-life of people in low-income countries. Other economists also developed indexes like Tobin and Nordhaus or Holub[22], but they proved to be either insufficient or too specific.

When assuming that growth leads to higher living standards, we can find several more arguments that are pro-growth. Higher living standards for a broad number of people lower crime and social conflict potential, because with higher satisfaction of needs there is no reason to steal and when a vast part of the society profits from prosperity, jealousy and thus inner social conflicts can be avoided.

Economic activity, more precisely economic activity after the industrial revolution, is undeniably a burden for the natural environment. The classical production process uses up natural resources and gives back waste products like carbon dioxide or atomic waste. These waste products can in the current huge scope never be absorbed and compensated by nature and leads thus to imbalances and destruction of our natural environment, which at the same time is our habitat. That is also why many leading scientists opt for internalizing these external effects into corporate finance to force the economy to change their habit. Refining our economic activity to a closed circle that recycles waste and does not produce products to be consumed but rather to be used is a crucial task for securing our own future.

The facts discussed in this chapter prove that economic growth is a very delicate task, which involves all members of a society and bears responsibility for current and coming generations. The political class as coordinator and regulator takes over a special role with responsibility for the entire society. That does not mean that this is only the politician's task. Society elects, in a democratic state, its representatives, who usually act according to the public opinion. Also companies produce by the consumer's demand. Consumers do have the power to force companies to produce sustainably for example. Companies on the other hand have the power to arouse demands with strategic marketing. All agents, society, economy, political class, form a dynamic whole and influence each other. They are only together able to achieve Oppenländer's pro-arguments, named above, and to avoid the contra-ones.

---

[22] Cf. Oppenländer (1988), p.173

2.4 Innovation

The title of this paper speaks of qualitative growth. The improvement of quality and living standard is almost always linked to an improvement in technology, which is based on innovation. We only need to look back in history to understand, how technological improvement has raised living conditions for millions and led to economic growth. The Industrial revolution in Europe was caused by progress in production capabilities. The English by that time had the mechanical loom and the steam engine, which gave them the opportunity of producing faster and with less effort a larger amount of products. The living standard of workers by that time had been admittedly bad, but social and political progress took care of that, so that nowadays, more than 150 years later, Europe, as part of the OECD, so a high-income region, is one of the world regions with the highest living standard and economically strong. Innovation played undeniably a crucial role in this progress and this role shall be propounded in this chapter.

Hitherto sophisticated knowledge has been concentrated in the USA, Japan and the EU, but the recent years have shown strong efforts by the emerging countries to build own knowledge pools and become less dependent on know-how from abroad, because it takes more than only producing more to obtain prosperity, it takes knowledge based economic growth.

Innovation is simply put the invention of technology[23], with technology being knowledge from all sciences.

Altenburg, Schmitz and Stamm elaborated three system approaches that capture an economy's ability to strive for becoming an innovative one[24].

The *Innovation systems approach*[25] describes the process of innovating as an interactive cycle. Research institutions, financed by public or private agents and often with an official mission, are the producers of knowledge and coordinate the research environment, foster a scientific community and distribute finances to specific projects eligible for funding. The official mission means in this case a formulated intention and the field of action. The German Helmholtz Association for example states that it wants to "contribute to solving grand challenges which face society, science and industry by performing top-rate research in

---

[23] Weil (2005), p.217
[24] Altenburg et al. (2007)
[25] Altenburg et al. (2007), p.5

strategic programs in the fields of Energy, Earth and Environment, Health, Key Technologies, Structure of Matter, Aeronautics, Space and Transport.[26]" These research institutions are research universities, foundations, institutes or science academies, like the German National Academy of Sciences Leopoldina, which conducts studies with the aim of advising the public and policy makers by studying important issues of global interest. The knowledge produced by the research institutions is put into practice or further used by the private sector. The approach assumes that stronger links between research institutions and private organizations lead to higher quality of the innovation system. Classically it assumed invention systems being limited or expanded to national borders, although the systems can exist in local and regional or international areas. From that can be concluded that innovation is dependent on geographical socio-cultural factors[27]. The innovation systems approach thus finds part of the explanation of why some countries have a high degree of knowledge while others do not. Admittedly the approach is insufficient when it comes to also considering cooperation between different, trans-regional networks and how they develop with the time.

That is exactly where the *Global value chain approach* steps in. It explains the development of former or actual low income countries, like China. Producing businesses have been strongly integrated and used in international value chains to manufacture simple finished products or components for foreign western or Hong-Kong Chinese companies. In that process the contractors, called *Lead Firms*[28], order these products and coordinate and supervise the production process. But in the course of that knowledge needs to be transferred to the suppliers, who can thus gain knowledge and benefit from this relationship. Contractors know of course about this and only provide information, where they really have to, so measurements or materials for example. The benefit is substantially stronger in the case of an acquisition. When a supplier is acquired it will no longer be a potential threat to its contractor's competitive advantage. Another case is, if one company acquires another one it simultaneously acquires its patents, knowledge, the contracts with skilled employees, licenses and so forth. What both cases prove is that the involvement into global value chains opens up opportunities for knowledge sourcing.

---

[26] Helmholtz Association (2012)
[27] Cf. Altenburg et al. (2007), p.5
[28] Cf. Altenburg et al. (2007), p.6

The approaches already discussed only consider institutions, so companies, universities, academies. But innovation is a man-made process and we thus need to complement the theory in adding the drivers of innovation: People.

The *Global professional network approach*[29] explains the impacts of the mobility of scientists. The German public currently discusses the phenomenon of skilled worker shortage and how to attract highly educated and skilled individuals, like engineers or natural scientists. These knowledge carriers do not always remain forever at the same place or institution. With new opportunities they become mobile, which can cause the so called "brain drain" or "brain circulation"[29]. The two terms are actually self-explaining. Drain is a leak, which means that things get lost in the one place and run to another one; in this specific case that is knowledge in terms of highly skilled individuals, who leave a country or region to live and work in another one. Altenburg and his co-authors state that brain drain has turned into brain circulation[29], which simply means that these highly skilled individuals travel frequently between regions and spread their contributions. Also return migration is a phenomenon of brain circulation. Parents from developing or emerging countries send their offsprings to classical countries that are strong in knowledge, like the USA, to study there. They become highly educated and return home, to China for example, and contribute here. It becomes obvious that these new mobile talents and the linkages, professional networks, they build up in the countries they are active in play a crucial role in building up innovation capabilities.

We can conclude that different analytical approaches need to be combined to capture innovation capabilities. Each of these approaches is insufficient in explaining the whole process of innovation and the construction of innovation capabilities. It is the interlocking action of all the described that presents us an overall picture. We learned that it takes tangible and intangible capital, which needs to be acquired to build up innovation capabilities. Necessary to create knowledge are research organizations, public and private, which work together interactively as well as agents that put knowledge into practice. But none of this would exist or work without talented and well-educated individuals. For these structures to emerge there must be a political and legal framework to protect intellectual property, determine and coordinate important research topics and activities and it takes a

---

[29] Cf. Altenburg et al. (2007), p.8

society, which appreciates and fosters learning and develops a value system to support the process of creating knowledge, of innovating.

2.5 How to measure innovation

Just like economic growth is innovation hard to measure and even harder to compare, because it is such a dynamic process, involving many intangible aspects, like the mind-set of society or the quality of scientific talent in a country, that capturing the whole is a difficult task – but feasible.

Comparing innovation capabilities is less difficult among very alike economies like the OECD countries, but then still the indicators chosen need to sufficiently informative.

There are some indicators that help interpreting the innovation capabilities of a country. These are *input indicators*[30] like the spending on research and development. This is usually depicted and thus comparable by the share of total GDP. Another input factor is human capital[30]. The amount of people graduating from universities and among them the achieved degrees say a lot about the quality of workforce in a country. Especially the number of PhDs is highly interesting, because these are the people creating new knowledge of importance. This newly created knowledge can be measured and compared by counting granted patents and published scientific papers. There are special indexes like the UNCTAD Innovation Capability Index and the Global Competitiveness Index, which we are going to use later, that are composed indicators, which represent the innovation capability of a country[31].

2.6 Prosperity and sustainable development

In 2.3 we named arguments for and against economic growth. One pro-argument states that growth is wealth-multiplying. This assumption is based on Adam Smith's theory, which says that growth leads to gain in wealth for every member of society[32]. Smith assumes that a gain in material possession automatically leads to a raise in prosperity or in other words makes everybody better-off. Exactly this way of thinking defined the way of acting in capitalist economies: Producing and having more leads to happiness. Oppenländer ascertains that human needs can never be satisfied for good[33] as the satisfaction of current needs leads to the evolvement of new ones and so on. And exactly this hunger for ever more is the driver of

---

[30] Altenburg et al. (2007), p.11
[31] Cf. Altenburg et al. (2007), p.13
[32] Oppenländer (1988), p. 171
[33] Cf. Oppenländer (1988), p.172

our capitalist economic system and the justification for economic growth. Not only the Club of Rome but also a growing share of the public realizes that having more is not sufficient in producing when it comes to creating happiness. Ever more people from emerging and developing countries are striving for having the same material wealth as the OECD countries - and they do have the right to. Shrinking natural resources, a tremendously damaged natural environment and climate change set limits to this hunger for more. That is why we need to shift our way of thinking and extend the perception of prosperity.

Prosperity most certainly includes material satisfaction. We need to eat, we need a roof over our heads, we need to dress, we want to be warm in winter, we want to be mobile and so forth and once these basic needs are met, we want more comfort, a nicer house, more fashionable clothes, more distinguished food. Expressed more simply: Bigger, better, faster, more.

In 1930 John Maynard Keynes published an essay called *Economic Possibilities for our Grandchildren*, in which he assessed that the generation of his grandchildren, meaning people living today in the OECD countries, will have to find a new way of economic acting, once the material scarcities, his generation faced, are overcome[34]. Keynes states that evolution made us human beings ever fighting for solving our economic scarcities, but once these are secured, we need to find new purposes in life. In other words: We need to find another qualitative content. Studies have shown that higher standard of living, so higher income does not make us automatically happier, as the following figure with the title "Subjective well-being by level of economic development" shows.

---

[34] Cf. Bundeszentrale für politische Bildung, Die wirtschaftlichen Möglichkeiten unserer Enkel, 29.08.2008

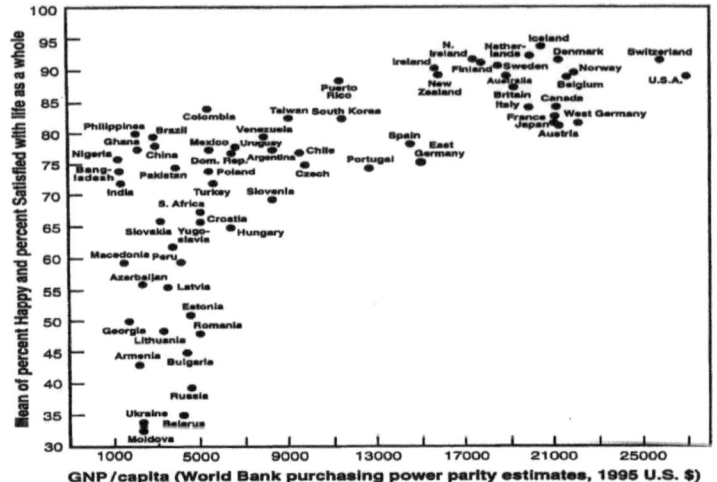

1: Subjective well-being by level of economic development

What we see here is that materially rich countries like Western Germany or Japan in 1995 were not significantly happier or more satisfied with their living conditions than people in low-income countries like Colombia or the Philippines. From these findings we can either conclude that people in rich countries are not happier, because of the ever newly arising demands, as we described above, which make them think, they still need more to finally become happy, or Keynes was wrong in his assumptions. He assumed that wealth will provide people more time for leisure but in fact people in industrialized countries today work just as much as 75 years ago[36]. The combination of these two assumptions explains the phenomenon. The deficiency of satisfaction of immaterial needs and the arising of ever new material demands makes people feel they are still not living under good conditions. That brings us to Tim Jackson, who adds a social dimension to the concept of prosperity[37].

The satisfaction of immaterial needs, as described in 2.3, is what makes life worth living besides material security. Being part of society and leading a meaningful life, where meaningful is widely and individually interpretable, is the key to true prosperity, says Jackson[37]. The social dimension of prosperity underlies ideological beliefs. It may include being loved or an accepted part of a social group, have an occupation that enables us to make a living, compassion and caring for others around us, live a self-determined life in

---

[35] Inglehart, R. and Klingemann, H.-D. (2000), Genes, culture, democracy and happiness
[36] Cf. Weil (2005), p.508
[37] Cf. Tim Jackson (2011), p.54

peace and so forth. These priorities are subject to cultural differences, religious beliefs and social structure. While a Westerner, for example, prefers striving for self-fulfillment, find indigenous cultures fulfillment in the happiness of the entire group. The ancient philosophy of Ubuntu even found its way into the current South African constitution. Ubuntu is a philosophy routed in southern African cultures and sees the individual as part of a whole, which vice versa means that the individual is nothing without the others around it. This philosophy stands for the values of sharing in a communal life with a harmonious togetherness[38].

The BBC commissioned GfK NOP in 2005 to conduct a study on the happiness of the British[39]. Question 15 is very informative: "And finally on this topic, please tell me in your own words, what Happiness is for you?" 47% answered that family and partnership constitute happiness, followed by health (24%). A comfortable home and financial security follow in obvious distance with 8 and 7%. The results prove the importance of the satisfaction of immaterial needs in a materially wealthy society like the one in the United Kingdom, the home of the industrial revolution.

We can thus conclude that the satisfaction of material needs only brings happiness up to a certain point. The concept of the diminishing marginal utility[40] of consumer goods displays that the more we own of a thing, the lesser the satisfaction we draw from it. That is where immaterial satisfaction steps in. The combination of economic and social aspects is what leads to prosperity. We can thus understand prosperity as the satisfaction of material and immaterial needs.

The often mentioned shrinking natural resources force us to reconsider how much and how we want to produce, if we plan to offer future generations the possibility of living in prosperity as well. Crude oil is such an example. We use it directly or indirectly for the production of the majority of products we consume, but the remaining reserves will be used up in roundabout 46 years[41]. But not only because of the emerging countries' economic rise demand for crude oil rose, the developed countries keep on consuming, so that young people from today are going to witness the end of the oil era, which will not leave a single

---

[38] Wikipedia (2012), a
[39] GfK NOP (2005), The Happiness Poll
[40] Cf. Jackson (2011), p.56
[41] British Petroleum (2009), World Energy Report

drop left for future generations. The following charts represent this phenomenon impressively.

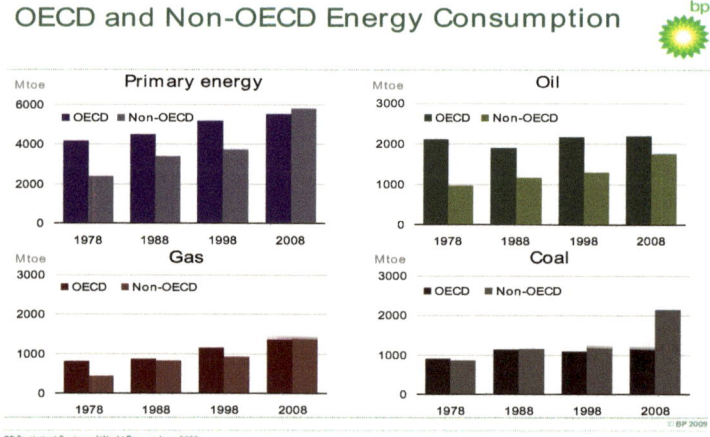

2 OECD and Non-OECD Energy Consumption

The steady rise on demand by the OECD-countries combined with the catching-up of the rest of the world are based on the exploitation of natural resources, which only exist in very limited amounts.

The sustainable way to prosperity is thus defined by a balanced approach that takes economic, social and ecologic aspects into consideration to ensure a survival as well as good, meaningful and free life for as many people as possible without excluding the same opportunities for future generations.

---

[42] British Petroleum (Ed.) (2009), World Energy Report

3. Striving for economic growth

In the previous chapters we discussed economic growth and its different components. We also said that measuring and analyzing the dynamic process of growth is a more than difficult task. But the theoretical instruments for that task exist.

3.1 Potential dynamics and structure dynamics

To analyze the growth process of an entire economy we normally make use of a basic formula that includes all factors leading to changes in the economy's output. The production function fulfills that purpose:

$C = f(L, K, R, T)$[43] with C being the economy's potential output, L labour capacity, K capital stock, R natural resources and T the technological capacity. The pure production function represents the potentially amount of available production factors so that we need to replace these by the actually used amounts and obtain:

$C_n = f(L_n, K_n, R_n, T_n)$[44], where C_n represents the economy's entire output with the respective factors used. Oppenländer excluded K and R for reasons of simplicity, but we shall still include them to show the entire factor group.

As this thesis shall not be primarily based on mathematical relations but observations and linkages between causalities, will we only lead the derivation to this point, as it explains the interrelations sufficiently.

This function's purpose is to enable us to analyze in detail how changes in a single factor change the overall output. The method of potential dynamics lets us scrutinize which factor caused economic changes[45]. The production factors are of course aggregated and sum up all resources belonging to that specific category.

Structure dynamics expound economic changes based on innovative changes instead of quantitative changes. This method is thus not primarily a quantitative but rather a qualitative analysis.

Oppenländer dismisses purely quantitative contemplations and thus the notion of proportional growth, meaning the output growing proportionally to the increase of input because an increase in output can not only be derived from increasing input factors, but

---

[43] Oppenländer (1988), p.5
[44] Cf Oppenländer (1988), p. 51
[45] Cf. Oppenländer (1988), p. 43

significantly from altering the factor combinations or improve factor quality[46]. That is why Oppenländer quotes furthermore that it is not an increase in production factors but an increase in growth factors that leads to economic growth. So simply hiring more workers does not automatically increase your output, but lending money, opening new markets or using new knowledge does[47], which brings us back to structural changes.

It can thus be concluded that the production function with the input factors does not sufficiently explain economic growth. First of all the factors cannot exactly be separated from one another and influence each other constantly directly and indirectly. A higher skilled work force for example can lead to technological progress through innovative ideas.

3.2 Qualitative Growth

Economic growth is thus a process that needs to be based on qualitative improvements in the long-run. Quantitative measurements, so increasing the number of input in the production process, is helpful to overcome scarcities in supply to the market, but it takes more to have a continuous process growth process.

David N. Weil tracks the causes of economic growth down to a change in productivity and found two reasons for it[48]. Technology and efficiency are the causes of an increase in productivity and thus economic growth.

It is true that also technological progress requires using resources. Engines and tools must be made of something and their development needs to be funded with financial resources, but technology has the very special characteristic of being somewhat non-rival. Technology, and that includes the know-how as well, can be used by many people at the same time. Technology does not necessarily explain, why there are rich and poor countries, but it does explain economic - qualitative - growth in the long-run[49].

Efficiency, so "how the available technology and inputs into production are actually used in producing output[50]", is the crucial structural management of resource allocation within an economy.

Qualitative growth means thus simply put: What do we make out of our available production factors? It means using production factors in such a way that output is maximized with

---

[46] Cf. Oppenländer (1988), p.52
[47] Cf. Oppenländer (1988), p.52
[48] Cf. Weil (2005), p.503
[49] Cf. Weil (2005), p.504
[50] Weil (2005), p.31

minimal input. Technological progress is the helper in thus process. Smart technology helps to minimize resource requirements. We already saw that happen in the Industrial Revolution, as described in the introduction to this paper. The spinning jenny for example made it possible to produce larger amounts of garments with less effort. Fewer workers were able to produce more. That is what technology must be aiming at. Using fewer resources, be it natural or financial resources, without lowering the economic output. That is exactly what qualitative growth means.

In the previous chapters we discussed GDP as the sum of all goods and services produced. What this concept does not take into consideration is the non-renewable natural resources used. This is an important fact as these resources will not be available for future generations and thus decrease the stock of natural capital as a production factor. For that reason Weil introduces the concept of *Green Gross Domestic Product*, which he defines as the usual notion of GDP "(the value of all the goods and services produced in a country in a given year) minus the value of natural capital that has been depleted or destroyed in that year.[51]" Obviously the result changes tremendously after having applied Green GDP. Especially countries, whose economy is based on natural resources, like the oil exporting countries, obtain a much lower GDP, as their economy is fueled by shrinking amounts of natural resources that do not regrow. The task of adding renewable resources to the calculation is rather complex. It is still easy when the amount of renewable resources used corresponds to the regrown amount. But if that resource is used to the extent that it cannot recover GDP falls. Natural degradation, like environmental pollution is almost impossibly to be priced, which makes the concept of Green GDP incomplete[52].

Using natural resources can make us materially better-off today, but what will future generations live on? In 1987 the United Nations Commission on Environment and Development, also known as the Brundtland Commission, stated that our economic acting must be designed in such a way that it "meets the needs of the present without compromising the ability of future generations to meet their needs.[53]" This defines the concept of *sustainable development*. What must be considered is to assign the right price to

---

[51] Weil (2005), p.473
[52] Weil (2005), p.477
[53] Weil (2005), p.472

the non-renewable resources, which is the in-ground-price, so the pure value of that resource before going through the value chain and obtaining a market price[54].

The definition makes it clear: We do not have to lower our standard of living today, but we have to make sure that future generations will not have to pay for our comfort by lowering their living standards. To continue the example of energy consumption we, for example, need to extend renewable energy sources to replace non-renewable, fossil ones. We thus have to use solar, wind and water power instead of nuclear or coal power plants. This way will also lead to an economic growth in creating a new sector with new jobs and new income. That is a sustainable way leading to prosperity.

---

[54] Cf. Weil (2005), p.476

4. China's economic rise – potentials and threats

The Chinese economy's output has grown on an average of 10 percent yearly since 1978 and if you take that year's index of real GDP 100 it grew to 1500.7 in 2007[55]. This is an extraordinary growth in economic output, especially compared to growth in OECD countries like Germany, who's GDP we calculated in 2.2. The rapid change becomes obvious, once you travel through China: The Jinghu High-Speed Railway takes four to five hours from Beijing to Shanghai - a distance of 1,318 km - where you can admire skyscrapers, German cars parking in front of luxury stores, you can go dine at gourmet restaurants or enjoy coffee in one of the countless Starbucks cafes. When you take the metro through Shanghai, you see people of all ages tapping and wiping their smartphones and tablet PCs. And all of that happened within three decades only. This chapter shall clarify how this change was made possible, what threatens the achievements and what needs to be done to prevent a loss in prosperity respectively how can sustainable prosperity be achieved.

4.1 Return of a world power
China can look back at four thousand years of rich cultural history as a dominating power that maintained trading contacts as far as to the African east coast. The invention of typography took place 700 years before Gutenberg, magnetic compass or gunpowder are only examples of Chinese genius, invented when Europeans only started their crusades to the Middle East[56].

When Deng Xiaoping took over power in December 1978 after having had to fight competitors from the so-called "Gang of Four", he inherited a country in a disastrous social and economic situation resulting from Mao's "Great Leap Forward" (1958-1960) and the "Cultural Revolution" (1966-1976)[57]. But Deng became famous for a package of reforms that form the base of the remarkable economic development the People's Republic of China experienced in the 20 years of his reign, which has changed the life of one fifth of the world population. He placed his loyal partners in official positions, which secured Deng two decades of enormous power and influence that helped him, putting his visions for China into practice. The crucial difference between Deng and his predecessors was that he focused on

---
[55] Chow (2010), p.26
[56] Cf. Seitz (2006), p.28 et seq.
[57] Wu (2012), p.8

following four areas to modernize: Agriculture, industry, science and technology instead of constructing a utopian Maoist society[58]. Deng started his reforms by liberating the agricultural production and returning farmland and the decisions about cultivation into private hand, which led to a remarkable increase in output[59]. This reform was followed by several others ranging from the sector of light industry to opening up to foreign trade partners.

The breakthrough came with Deng's travel through the south of China in early 1992. This journey led him from Shanghai via Wuhan to the special economic zone of Shenzhen, where he proclaimed that the Communist Party of China (CPC) must focus on fostering China's economic progress in accelerating reforms and opening up economically to partners from overseas[60].

Deng's political acting was based on the following important principles: Socialism means fostering workers, foreign investors are a useful help, prosperity can only be achieved step by step so that the people has to accept inequalities. Taiwan, Singapore and others serve as role models[61]. The most important principle is said with Deng's phrase "It doesn't matter whether it's a white cat or a black, I think; a cat that catches mice is a good cat.[62]", which he already said in 1961. This underlines Deng's pragmatism. He neglects ideology for the sake of progress. Deng thus established a new way of Chinese governance that led China to the position of one of today's world powers.

To scrutinize the origins of China's growth we shall have another look at the production function: $C = f(L, K, R, T)$. The empirical application of this function to the real developments in China is obviously not precisely possible, but interpretations of correlations are feasible.

The large availability of cheap labor forces is undeniably one of China's largest assets. The vast amount of low skilled and thus low-paid workers combined with the low price level in China made and still make the country an attractive place for foreign-owned and also Chinese-owned production plants, especially in labor intensive manufacturing processes. The following table published by the US American Bureau of Labor Statistics shows the compensation costs of manufacturing workers on an hourly basis in comparison to the OECD and emerging countries:

---

[58] Cf. Seitz (2006), p.232
[59] Cf. Seitz (2006), p.236
[60] Cf. Seitz (2006), p.299
[61] Seitz (2006), p.300 et seq.
[62] Wikipedia (2012), b

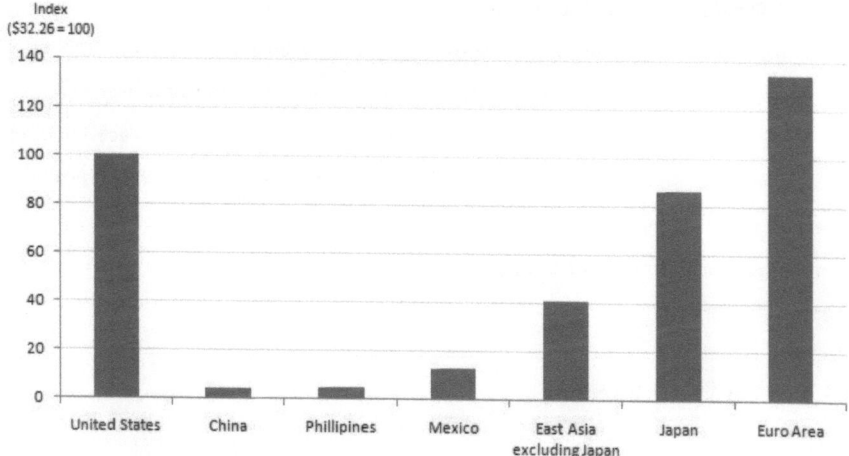

SOURCE: U.S. Bureau of Labor Statistics, Division of International Labor Comparisons

3 Hourly compensation costs of manufacturing employees in selected economies and regions[63]

The gap in labor compensation between OECD countries and China cannot be made more obvious and makes China an almost incompetable production place attracting foreign direct investment (FDI) and thus an inflow of foreign exchange.

These incoming currencies are directly converted into the Chinese currency Renminbi (RMB), which increases the amount of money circulating in the Chinese economy and causes banks lending it on low interest rates, so that the money keeps on streaming into the Chinese economy[64]. The supply with cheap money leads in the short run to an increase in economic output, stated the renowned economist Milton Friedman in the 1930s, but later leads to inflation, so a rise in price-level, at a later stage[65]. This observation has proven to be true for China as well and led to the effect, today known as the "over-heated" Chinese economy.

Up until 2002 money supply by the Chinese central bank, the People's Bank of China, and the economic output rose at the same pace, but then began to undock: Between 2002 and 2005 the amount of RMB emitted rose with rates of 0.0965, 0.1335, 0,836 and 0.1128, but real GDP only increased by 0.087, 0.096, 0.96 and 0.97 in the same period of time (as measured

---

[63] U.S. Bureau of Labor Statistics, Division of International Labor comparisons (2008), Hourly compensation costs of manufacturing employees in selected economies and regions, 2008
[64] Cf. Chow (2010), p.90
[65] Chow (2010), p.89

by the GDP deflator)⁶⁶. The discrepancy becomes obvious. There was and still is more money circulating than real counter values existing respectively arising. But cheap money will continue overheating the economy, because of the tremendous inflow of foreign currencies. The artificially low exchange rate of the RMB makes China an attractive place for foreign direct investment, so the inclusion into the global value chain, and fosters China's position as an export world champion, as Chinese products are so much cheaper compared to products from Europe for example. We are going to learn about this phenomenon in the following chapter.

4.2 Threats to China's prosperity

The growth of the Chinese economy as described above is based on feet of clay. Cheap money, an export based economy depending on foreign trade partners, social and political tensions threaten China's wealth and thus the achievements of the past thirty years.

The exchange rate of the Chinese RMB is artificially kept low. Usually a currency's exchange rate is linked to the market forces of supply and demand. If foreigners buy lots of products from Germany for example, another very strong exporter, the value of its currency rises due to the strong demand for it, as we could see happening with the Deutsche Mark. Today we can witness a currency war between the USA and China: China wants to keeps its currency cheap so that the world keeps on buying in China. But the USA want to sell their products too and thus lower the base rate of the US Dollar to almost zero percent to make the Dollar cheaper. But that does neither solve China's problem of inflowing foreign exchange, nor does it sufficiently solve America's economic difficulties⁶⁷. Economies have the opportunity of choosing to have a fixed or a floating exchange rate system. The advantage of a fixed exchange rate system is that easing money supply does not influence the currency's value too negatively compared to other currencies. The disadvantage is that the country hands over control over its own monetary system to the authorities of the currency it is linked to – usually the US Dollar. China is not forced to choose either or, but can decide to compromise, as will be explained in 4.3.

We mention the large Chinese population here, because it is apparently seen as a potential threat to China's prosperity by Chinese officials, which made them introduce strict birth control laws. Analysts contradict by arguing that the national and world food supply as well

---

⁶⁶ Chow (2010), p.90
⁶⁷ Cf. Chow (2010), p.91

as pure geographical space in the country is sufficient to feed and lodge the Chinese population[68]. Also the natural population growth rate decreased from 12 percent in 1978 to 5.17 percent in 2007[69]. This slowed down the pace by which the Chinese people grows, but will certainly lead to an over-aged society and rising care costs. The birth control leads thus to a new threat to China's wealth in trying to avoid another one.

Accepting differences and inequalities on the path to prosperity is what Deng demanded. His reforms made people generally better off compared to the Mao-years, but now there is a large number of people that becomes rich very quickly, while others remain in a vicious cycle of poverty. Especially the rural population, of which many earn their living as migrant workers, does not benefit from the economic growth. The average per capita income of people living and working in cities in 2011 was 6977 RMB, while rural workers earned 2963 RMB in that same year[70]. Most of the migrant workers lost their jobs in farming due to new and more efficient technologies and thus move through the country looking for short term employment in the fields of manufacturing or construction, leaving older relatives and children behind in the villages they came from. But this sharp income inequality is explosive. In 2011 there were in total 252.78 million migrant workers[71]. They see and feel the inequality daily and thus start asking for improvement of their situation. That is why the Chinese government raises their average income yearly, but money is not everything. These workers want to send their children to school, they want to become official residents of the regions they work in and they want to settle down and obtain security in life, they want to satisfy their immaterial needs. Those are problems the Chinese officials will have to solve soon to prevent social instability.

Natural resources are often no assets in the sense of belonging to someone. They are thus free to use without paying for it. That unfortunately leads to companies overusing natural resources like water. Also air pollution and poisoned groundwater are crucial issues. China's leadership recognized that problem and first published its White Paper on Environmental Protection in 2006[72]. This report covers the year 1996 to 2005 and displays the Chinese measures taken to fight environmental damages in for example rural and metropolitan areas, damages caused by industrial production. Remarkable is that the Chinese are aiming

---

[68] Cf. Chow (2010), p.171 et seq.
[69] Chow (2010), p.173
[70] National Bureau of Statistics of China (2012), a
[71] National Bureau of Statistics of China (2012), b
[72] Cf. china.org.cn, White Paper on Environmental Protection Published, June 5, 2006

at industrializing nature protection and thus seek to invest heavily in the respective fields of technology, as they describe in the White Paper's chapter IX.

We mentioned earlier that production in China is still dominated by simple products and production processes. Foreign companies outsource production of simple components to China and also Chinese companies still need to catch up in technology as described in 2.4. China ranks very low in global comparison of production process sophistication. The Global Competitiveness Report analyzed production processes in 139 countries, where China is put on rank 55 with an index of 3.9[73]. To better understand this number: Japan is on rank one with an index of 6.6 followed by Germany with 6.5. China is also often compared to India, which was ranked 43rd with an index of 4.3. That shows very clearly that China still needs to work hard on further developing its technological capacities to make sure its economic growth lasts in the long-run.

4.3 China's potential for sustainable prosperity

To strive for sustainable prosperity, China needs to overcome the obstacles expounded in the previous chapter.

To solve its internal problem of an overheated economy, China must moderately raise the exchange rate of its RMB to the market equilibrium, so make the RMB more expensive compared to other foreign currencies[74]. That solution is going to cool the Chinese economy down to normal temperatures, to stay in the picture, and demand for Chinese products is not going to decrease significantly as China is already too integrated in the world economy and has made it somewhat irreplaceable.

The large and willing Chinese population is certainly a potential and must be integrated in the growth process wisely and respectfully. The Chinese men and women are more than simply workers and when trained right and given the opportunity to act freely, they can contribute crucially to the Chinese growth process. So far this process has been managed centrally by the Government in Beijing, but smart entrepreneurs, engineers and skilled workers will contribute their bit in creating new businesses, technological progress and form a motivated workforce. When real chances are good for the vast majority of the Chinese to ascend to the middle class and create an own little wealth, people will work hard for it and social peace will be preserved. But for that justice, fairness, equal chances and rights must

---

[73] Schwab, K (2010), The Global Competitiveness Report 2010 – 2011, Data Tables, a
[74] Cf. Chow (2010), p.92

be central values of the Chinese society. The Chinese population as a whole is thus the key factor: A functioning society brings forth smart people contributing to a common goal, values like social togetherness and environmental awareness. The society itself must be sensitized to being the key to sustainable prosperity.

The central government is now to be seen as a potential, because China has no democratic tradition and necessary measures can be taken quicker than when having to consult elected representatives of 1.3 billion Chinese. In the long-run exactly this will become a threat as well, because the government willingly hindered a dynamic society in ruling in a top-down way and thus political opening and easing are necessary in the long-run, as we are going to learn in the coming chapter.

4.4 Interpretation and outlook

Many of the threats to Chinese prosperity are based on political and social problems. China thus needs to strive for social progress, which means that all members of that society "work and live happily as they themselves recognize that they are living and working happily[75]". Therefor basic material needs, as we described in 2.3, need to be satisfied, because living and misery will certainly never make people consider themselves as living good. Also the society should provide justice as well as "law and order[76]", so the satisfaction of immaterial needs.

China undergoes several transformations at the same time. Deng Xiaoping started to transform the Chinese economy into a market economy. This is a first step towards a prosperous society in terms of what we defined in chapter 2.6. But political reforms need to follow to serve the growing demand for self-determination and participation. Observers of Chinese politics are sure that the time for political liberalization will come as soon as the Chinese society is ready for the new step. The Chinese know very well that Gorbatchov's Glasnost and Perestroika led to the difficult economic and political situation Russia faces nowadays and thus the Chinese officials decided to start with economic reforms followed by political ones.

The Chinese success – economically, politically and societal - , despite its problems, proves that the Chinese way is appropriate for the country and the Chinese society.

---

[75] Chow (2010), p.65
[76] Chow (2010), p.66

5. Conclusion

The continuous and fast catching-up process of the BRICS countries, Brazil, Russia, India, China and South Africa, astonishes the rest of the world and leads a growing share of the world population towards prosperity. With that the world's wealth starts being spread more just, while in the past the rich countries have been European and northern American ones.

The gap between so-called rich and poor countries is nonetheless still large. The per capita income of the world's richest countries outdoes the per capita income of the poorest by the factor of 40[77]. People living in those low-income countries still do not have sufficient access to the sources that enable them to satisfy their basic needs, so food, clean water, proper housing, health care and safety. Western societies have long succeeded in sustainably ensuring the satisfaction of these basic needs, but still people in these societies do not perceive themselves as being happy as was expounded in 2.6. The difference is that high-income and low-income countries are on different levels of development. High-income countries, today the OECD-countries, managed to increase their economic output in a way that all material needs can be satisfied and indeed over-satisfied. But as John M. Keynes already found in 1930 will these societies have to figure out how to become happy in the sense of satisfying their immaterial needs and still preserving their prosperity. Low-income countries must still get to that point and first need to find a way to overcome the material scarcities they face today or in other words increase their economic output to create income for as many people as possible.

The way to increasing economic output is economic growth. This is not only managed by producing more, but also by producing smarter. First of all one has to produce more, when there is a scarcity. When people are starving because there is not enough bread, then more bread needs to be produced to appease the hunger. But this quantitative approach has its limits. Once there is enough bread for everyone, once the material need for food is satisfied, people demand better food. They want meat, they want cake and they want a variety of food to choose from. The satisfaction of one material demand leads thus to new demands and will in the end never lead to happiness. Thus immaterial needs have to be taken into consideration. To be happy we want to be accepted and respected part of a social group, we

---

[77] Weil (2005), p.502

want to be free and live self-determined. The combination of the satisfaction of material and immaterial needs leads thus to true prosperity.

It is not only that material needs can never be ultimately satisfied, it is also that shrinking natural resources force us to find new ways of production. Production processes must become more efficient and thus more innovative to increase productivity without increasing the resource input at the same scale the output increases. The structural management of resource allocation defines efficiency as described in chapter 3.2 and leads to qualitative growth. The instrument is innovation. Innovation comprises the creation of new knowledge, which is then used for the progression of the technological way of working and producing.

That is exactly the phase China is in right now. The People's Republic has seen tremendous increases in economic output and growing wealth for a growing number of people. This was made possible by first leading the masses of people out of hunger and material deficiency, which the Mao era caused. Deng Xiaoping liberalized agricultural production and thus increased the output in this sector. He also opened the Chinese market to foreign investors and pushed production in selected sectors forward. But economic growth in China is based on feet of clay: Cheap workforce, strong exploitation of natural resources and social inequalities enabled the remarkable increase in output that China witnessed in the past 20 to 30 years.

That way Chinese products were unbeatably cheap on the world market, which made China the most attractive production place for foreign, especially Western companies, but will not be able to ensure prosperity in the long-run. Because of its attractiveness for FDI China was able to accumulate large amounts of foreign currencies and benefited from technology transfer. This financial blessing enabled China to invest selectively in key sectors. The spending on research and development has increased by 20% per year since 1999 and amounted to 1.3% of GDP in 2005[78]. This heavy investment combined with technology transfer because of international cooperation led to technological progress in China. The role of foreign direct investment on the field of technological innovation is also shown in the statistics of the Global Competitiveness Report. The question here was: "To what extent does foreign direct investment (FDI) bring new technology into your country?[79]" with 1 meaning "not at all" and 7 "FDI is a key source of new technology". The result for China is a

---

[78] Altenburg et al. (2007), p.11
[79] Schwab, K. (2010), The Global Competitiveness Report 2010 – 2011, Data Tables, b

weighted average of 5.1, which proves the importance of the inflow of knowledge and technology from abroad.

The Chinese government knows about the risks of depending so strongly on foreign trade partners because they might run out of money and will thus stop buying Chinese products but also because they understandably never fully disclose their know-how. That is why the National People's Congress underlined the importance of own knowledge creation in the current Twelfth Five Year Plan: "Scientific progress and innovation will support the transformation. Through comprehensively implementing the strategy of rejuvenating our country through science and education and talents, we will give full play to the role of science and human resources. China should upgrade its capabilities in indigenous research and innovation in science, technology and administration, train more innovative talents and improve education for workers. In a word, we will strive to speed up the construction of an innovation country[80]". This way is going to slow down economic growth, but will at the same time make growth and the gained prosperity more sustainable. Qualitative growth ensures that also in the future there will be sufficient resources to feed the economic activities and fostering the workforce eases social tensions, which makes the Chinese society more stable and harmonic. A higher skilled workforce will earn a higher income, which is also a way of satisfying immaterial needs and material needs, of killing two birds with one stone. The Chinese government has obviously recognized the necessary steps to striving for sustainable prosperity:

Sustainable prosperity can be achieved through qualitative growth, which means to not simply increase economic output with quantitative measures, but increase productivity through efficiency and innovation. Economic growth is a political task with a dominating social dimension because the economy shall always only be a tool for human beings to create wealth, overcome material scarcities respectively to satisfy material and immaterial needs.

Sustainable prosperity through qualitative economic growth is thus achievable when balancing economic, social and ecologic aspects to ensure survival as well as good, meaningful and free life for as many people as possible without excluding the same opportunities for future generations.

---

[80] National People's Congress (2011), Twelfth Five Year Plan (2011-2015), Chapter 2: Guiding Principles

List of References

Altenburg, T., Schmitz, H., Stamm, A. (2007), Breakthrough? China's and India's Transition from Production to Innovation, Bonn and Sussex

British Petroleum (Ed.) (2009), World Energy Report

Bundeszentrale für politische Bildung (29.08.2008), Die wirtschaftlichen Möglichkeiten unserer Enkel, on the internet: URL: Http://www.bpb.de/veranstaltungen/-WBTJ4S,0,0, Die_wirtschaftlichen_M%F6glichkeiten_unserer_Enkel.html

Chow, G. (2010), Interpreting China's Economy, Singapore

China.Org (Ed.) (05.07.2006), White Paper on Environmental Protection Published

The Club of Rome (2012), on the internet: URL: http://www.clubofrome.org

Coen, A. (02.12.2011), 40,9 Prozent sind schon glücklich , Zeit Online, on the internet: URL: http://www.zeit.de/2011/49/Kapitalismuskritik-Bhutan

GfK NOP (2005), The Happiness Poll

Helmholtz Association (2012), Mission of the Helmholtz Association, on the internet: URL: http://www.helmholtz.de/en/about_us/mission/

Inglehart, R. and Klingemann, H.-D. (2000), Genes, culture, democracy and happiness

Jackson, T. (2012), Wohlstand ohne Wachstum : Leben und Wirtschaften in einer endlichen Welt, München

National Bureau of Statistics of China (Ed.) (2012), on the internet: URL: http://www.stats.gov.cn/english

    a Income of Urban and Rural Residents in 2011

    b Statistical Communiqué of the People's Republic of China on the 2011 National Economic and Social Development[1]

National People's Congress (Ed.) (2011), Twelfth Five Year Plan (2011-2015), Chapter 2: Guiding Principles

Oppenländer, K. (1988), Wachstumstheorie und Wachstumspolitik, München

Schwab, K. (2010), The Global Competitiveness Report 2010 – 2011, Data Tables

    a Production process sophistication

    b FDI and technology transfer

Seitz, K. (2006), China – Eine Weltmacht kehrt zurück, München

United Nations Organization (Ed.) (2012), Human Development Reports, on the internet:
URL: http://hdr.undp.org/

U.S. Bureau of Labor Statistics, Division of International Labor comparisons (2008), Hourly compensation costs of manufacturing employees in selected economies and regions, 2008

Weil, D. (2005), Economic Growth, Boston

Wikipedia (Ed.) (2012), on the internet: URL: http://de.wikipedia.org

a Ubuntu (Philospohie), 19.07.2012

b Deng Xiaoping 24 October 2012

The World Bank Group (Ed.) (2012), on the internet: URL: http://data.worldbank.org/

a How we classify countries
b GDP (current US$)

Wu, Y. (2012), Understanding Economic Growth in China and India, Singapore

Zabel, U. (2011),) Lecture: Ökologische Unternehmenspolitik